The Luck Child

A new retelling of an Irish folktale

Written by Malachy Doyle
Illustrated by Laura Anderson

Turn to page 21 for
Moya and the Little Red Bull

Pearson Australia
(a division of Pearson Australia Group Pty Ltd)
707 Collins Street, Melbourne, Victoria 3008
PO Box 23360, Melbourne, Victoria 8012
www.pearson.com.au

Story by Malachy Doyle
Illustrated by Laura Anderson
Designed by Bigtop

First published 2011 by Pearson Education Limited
This edition published 2012 by Pearson Australia
2019 2018 2017 2016
10 9 8 7 6 5 4 3 2

Printed in Australia by the SOS Print - Media Group

ISBN 978 1 4425 5728 4

Pearson Australia Group Pty Ltd
ABN 40 004 245 943

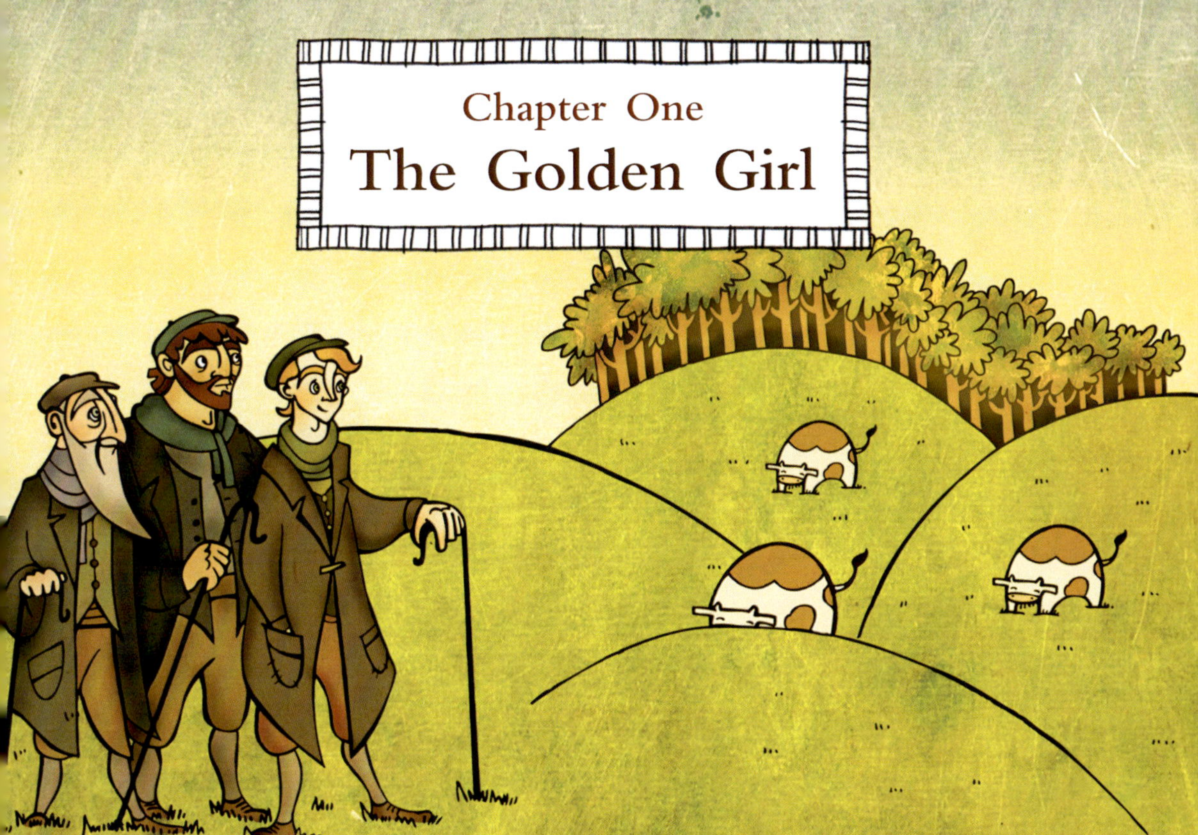

Chapter One
The Golden Girl

Aidan, Brian and Conary looked after the cows of the High King of Ireland.

Aidan was old and wise, Brian was young and fierce, and Conary had a heart as soft as a feather pillow.

Their job was to keep the wild beasts away from the king's cows, so at night they slept in little wicker huts on the edge of the deep, dark forest.

One day, as Conary was gathering wood for the fire, he heard a tiny cry. Following the sound to the foot of a tree, he found a beautiful baby girl wrapped in a golden blanket.

As he picked her up, the little girl smiled at him, and Conary felt as happy as he'd ever been in his life.

"What have you got there?" asked Brian. Conary tried to hide the little girl, but Brian saw her.

"This is no place for a child!" he said. "I don't know where she came from, Conary, but you'll have to get rid of her."

The baby peeped out from under Conary's coat and smiled up at Brian, melting even his fierce heart.

Old Aidan arrived at that moment and saw the baby girl, wrapped in her beautiful blanket.

"This is no ordinary child," he said, looking at her closely. "She is a princess of a distant land. You may keep her for now, Conary, but be warned! She's been stolen by the Little People, who live deep under the ground."

Conary gasped. "Why did they steal her, Aidan, and why have they left her here?"

"Their own children are all wrinkled and wizened," explained Aidan, "so they come up to the surface, when the moon is shining clear, seeking out the prettiest little humans to brighten up their darkness. She's their Luck Child and, as sure as there are stars in the sky, they'll be back for her once she's grown."

"She's too beautiful and good for the Little People!" cried Conary. "I'll call her Moya and take care of her, and she'll bring me luck and happiness."

"I'll help you, Conary," said Brian, quietly. "For she smiled at me, and there's not many who do that."

The baby opened her eyes again and saw Aidan's wrinkled old face looking down at her. She smiled up at him, too, and won his ancient heart.

Chapter Two
Three Wishes

Aidan, Brian and Conary found a secret place, deep in the depths of the forest. They made a hut for Moya, where she'd be safe from the Little People and from the wild animals, too, and took it in turns to look after her.

Year by year, Moya grew, until she was no longer a baby but a pretty young girl.

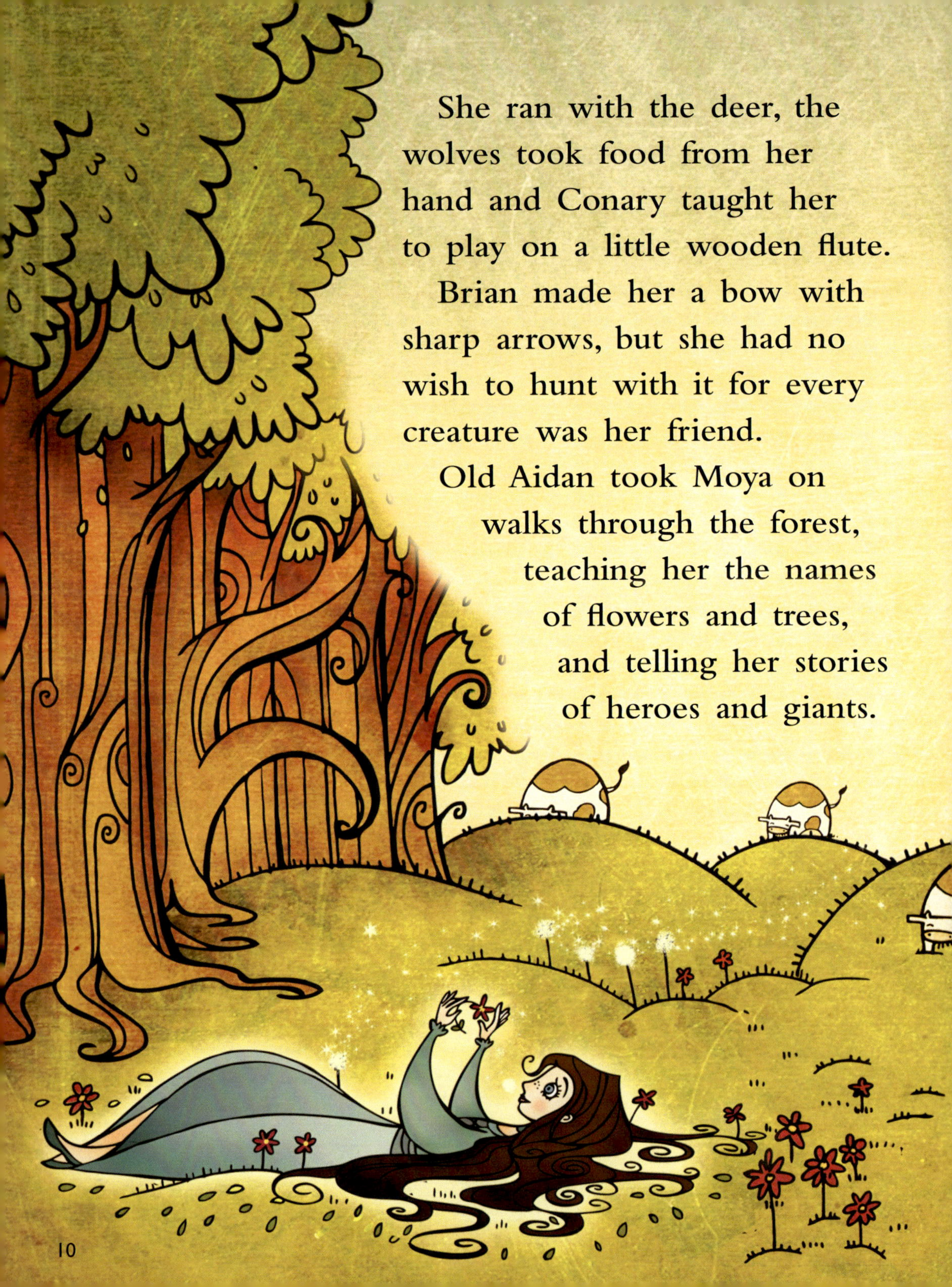

She ran with the deer, the wolves took food from her hand and Conary taught her to play on a little wooden flute.

Brian made her a bow with sharp arrows, but she had no wish to hunt with it for every creature was her friend.

Old Aidan took Moya on walks through the forest, teaching her the names of flowers and trees, and telling her stories of heroes and giants.

One morning, Aidan found Conary out guarding the cows, with the saddest look on his face.

"Moya's growing up so fast," said his friend. "Soon the Little People will find out that she's no longer a child. They might take her away and make her their queen."

"They won't get her without a fight!" shouted Brian, rushing over.

"There'll be no fighting," Aidan told him. "We look after Moya as well as we can, for as long as we can. She brings us joy, and one day she'll give each of us our heart's wish."

"I'd wish for a golden coat, like the blanket she came in, so that I could always feel her close to me," said Conary.

"I'd wish for a silver spear and a golden shield," cried Brian, "to defeat any enemy!"

"I'd ask to sit in the king's castle with her and hear the poets praise her," said old Aidan.

Young Moya came skipping by and, when they told her of their wishes, she laughed.

"Well, I'd wish never to have to leave the forest and my three lovely friends!" she said.

Chapter Three

The Little People and the King

One night, under the fullness of the moon, the Little People came calling.

"Where's the Luck Child?" they cried at the door.

"She's sleeping. Please don't take her!" begged Conary.

"Bring out the Luck Child!" they shrieked again and again.

“Clear off!” yelled Brian. “You can’t have her!”

“That’s no way to speak to the Little People,” said old Aidan, going outside. “I’m afraid Moya’s not quite ready for you yet, gentlemen,” he told them. “Why not come back in a year?”

“Fair enough,” said their leader, for he liked how Aidan had spoken to them. “You’d better not be tricking us, though!”

The next morning, the three men were out collecting wood when a jet-black dog ran through the trees.

"It's the king's dog!" said Aidan. "Run for the hut, Moya, and hide before you're seen!"

She tried to escape, but the dog caught hold of her dress and she couldn't move.

The King of Ireland rode up on his mighty horse. "Who is this?" he asked, looking first at Moya and then at the three men. "I can see she's none of yours, for she's far too pretty!"

“Her name is Moya, sir,” said Conary. “We found her in the woods when she was a baby. We’ve always taken good care of her, and in return she brings us joy and luck.”

“Well, she’d better come with me then,” said the king, “for there’s talk of war in the land, and I’m more in need of luck than you three are.”

“I’ll go with you if I must, my lord,” said Moya. “Aidan, Brian and Conary have been good to me, though. Would you grant them each a wish?”

“I’ll do what I can, child,” said the king. “What would you like for them?”

"Well ..." The girl thought long and hard. "I'd like a golden coat for gentle Conary, to remind him of me and to keep him warm out here in the forest ..."

"I'd like a silver spear and golden shield for Brian the brave, and for you to make him one of your guards ..." she continued.

"Most of all I want my lovely, kind Aidan, who's really too old now to be looking after your cattle, to come and live with me in your castle and tell me stories."

"You shall have everything you ask for and more," said the king.

So Brian was allowed to join the king's guard, he and Conary got their gold and silver, and they were both made very welcome whenever they wished to visit Aidan and Moya.

Moya was given a beautiful room in the king's castle, looking out over her beloved forest. She was safe there from the Little People, for there was a wall of magic around the royal kingdom, preventing them from ever entering.

The poets sang her praises, the queen loved her as a daughter and, thanks to the Luck Child, all talk of war was gone, and Ireland was at peace for a thousand years.

Moya, the Luck Child

Moya and the Little Red Bull

A re-invention of 'The Small Red Bull', a traditional Irish folktale

Written by Malachy Doyle
Illustrated by Laura Anderson

Chapter One
The Jealous Queen

The King of Ireland's wife had been sick for a long time, and one day she passed away.

The king was as lonely as lonely could be and, believing that Moya needed a mother, he sought a new wife. The woman he married, though, had three sons already – Cucadoo, Cucadee and Cucadiddle.

The new queen was jealous of how fond the king was of Moya, so she decided to do away with her.

Every morning she sent her off to mind the cattle in the king's fields, but did she give Moya any breakfast? She did not! Did she give her any food for the day? She did not!

Was Moya starving when she got home? Certainly not! Was she wasting away with hunger? Not a bit!

"Cucadoo ..." the woman called to her youngest son. "Go with that good-for-nothing Moya and find out what she's eating!" So he did.

They went to the fields together to mind the cows, and when the midsummer sun was high in the sky, Moya sang, "It's time to chew, Cucadoo!"

She ran up the hill and did a handstand at the top.

Then she somersaulted back down, picking two leaves of sorrel as she went and popping one in her mouth.

When she got to the bottom she gave the other to the boy and, as soon as he nibbled it, he fell asleep.

"Little bull, little bull!" cried Moya, as soon as Cucadoo's eyes had closed.

Up trotted the little red bull and struck one of its horns on the ground. Out of the horn came a table and a chair. On the table was every type of food you might ever wish for!

Moya ate and drank to her heart's content, before the little bull put everything back into its horn and trotted off to join the other cattle.

Chapter Two
Moya's Secret

"What did you see the girl eat?" asked the boy's mother, when they got home.

"Just a leaf," said Cucadoo.

"A single leaf?" she cried. "Don't be ridiculous!"

So she told her middle son, Cucadee, to go with Moya the next day.

At noon Moya yelled, "Time to climb a tree, Cucadee!"

She raced to the highest oak tree, clambered up it, and picked the two topmost leaves. Then she hurried back down and leapt to the ground.

When she came to a halt at Cucadee's feet, she ate a leaf, gave the other to the boy, and what do you think happened then?

He fell asleep, the little bull came, and Moya feasted.

“Cucadoo was right, Mother,” said Cucadee when he got home. “All she had to eat was a single oak leaf.”

“Don’t be stupid, boy!” the woman snorted. “You can’t live on leaves!”

“I’ll go tomorrow, Mother,” said Cucadiddle, the eldest son. “Then we’ll find out what she’s eating, once and for all.”

“Time to fiddle, Cucadiddle!” said Moya, when the sun was high in the sky.

She skipped all around, in and out of the hedges. Then she ran back with two blackthorn sticks, rubbing one against the other till the sweetest music came out.

Moya danced a little jig, picked two mint leaves and offered one to the boy.

But ...

"None for me, thanks," said Cucadiddle, opening his bag. "I've bread and milk here and they'll do me fine."

He didn't eat the mint, so he didn't fall asleep. He didn't fall asleep, so Moya couldn't call the bull.

But the little bull was lonely. It trotted up to Moya, and before she could stop it …

it tapped a horn on the ground and out came the table and the food.

"Aha!" cried Cucadiddle. "Wait till Mother hears about this!"

Chapter Three
The Handsome Prince

"That girl's tricking us!" hissed the woman, when Cucadiddle told her. "Well, two can play at that game!" So she took herself to bed, pretending to be sick.

"Shall I fetch the doctor?" asked the king, coming in.

"It's too late for doctors," gasped his wife. "The only thing that'll save me now is a cup of beef soup from that little red bull of yours. You'll have to kill it and make me some."

The king shook his head. "Moya would never forgive me!"

would you rather it was ME who was dead?
moaned the queen.

"I'll do it in the morning, then," sighed her husband.

He went and told Moya, Moya went and told the bull, and the two of them ran away into the night.

They raced and they magically galloped, all the way to the castle of the King of Scotland.

“Have you come to marry my son?” said the king.

“Maybe,” said Moya, surprised.

“Well, I’ll tell you what,” said the king, “you can have a meal and a good night’s sleep but then you’re to hide, young lady – and if you’re found, you’re in trouble. Big trouble!”

“If you haven’t found me by sunset tomorrow, what happens then?” asked Moya. She could see the handsome young prince smiling over at her and, liking the look of him, she thought it might be worth the risk.

“You can marry my son, if he’s willing,” said the king.

Chapter Four
Moya's Hiding Place

"Where will I hide?" Moya asked the little red bull, and the bull looked up, high.

So Moya climbed on his back and bounced up and down. The bull bucked, Moya flew through the air, and she landed on the flagpole at the very top of the castle and hung on for dear life, all day.

The king's men hunted her up and down, in and out. Did they spot her? They did not. Did they harm her? They did not.

So Moya married the King of Scotland's only son. He was happy, she was happy, and so was the little red bull.